Custom Code Cash

~ The Complete Website Custom Coding Lecture Series ~
First Edition

~ *Table of Contents* ~

Patti Markow

Lecture 1 - Introduction

Hi!

My name is Patti Markow and I'll be your guide as we traverse through the magically fun world of custom website coding. By the end of this lecture series you will be able to custom code your own websites and be equipped with all of the links, resources and services you will need to create your own enterprise.

My origin in computer programming was pre-internet. I was a COBOL programmer, which does not exist anymore. Using the basic programming techniques I knew, I was able to translate my knowledge into website coding. I program websites in, and will teach you, basic HTML (Hyper Text Mark-up Language), PHP, Mysql (database) and a little Javascript.

I know that this all sounds a little intimidating at first, but programming a website is relatively easy to learn. I will present these lectures in as much plain language as possible and will assume you are totally unfamiliar with any kind of programming. If you do have some knowledge, you may be able to skip a few of the lectures or, perhaps, just use this manual as a reference.

And what I've included with your purchase of the Custom Code Cash lecture series is free access to the Custom Code Cash online course where you will find, in one place, all of the information and links you will need to begin your custom coding experience - along with sample sites and website template, where I have pre-coded a basic website. All you have to upload the template to your web host, follow instructions and fill in the blanks.

You can access the online Custom Code Cash course here:

http://www.customcodecash.com/started.php

Lecture 2 - A Basic Website

A basic website is one or more HTML documents that are able to be accessed on the internet because the document files are hosted on internet servers. Generally speaking, you are able to rent use of internet servers through a web hosting company.

Even at this writing, there are probably already billions of individual websites accessible on the internet. Every one of these websites has a unique www (world wide web) address, or URL. To view a website, using your web browser, you type the unique URL into the address bar. For a website to have a unique URL, the website owner must register a domain name and associate his website files with the directory for the domain.

www.uniquedomain.com - this is an example of a URL.
uniquedomain.com - this is an example of a domain name.
.com - is the extension of the domain.

When you want to register a domain for a website, you must first use a tool to search the realm of all existing domains to see if it is available. If it is, you can register the domain and you become the owner of the domain. To register a domain you must provide personal information, such as your full name or company name, physical address, phone number and email address. Once registered, this information is readily accessible by anyone who wants it unless you purchase domain privacy. When you purchase domain privacy, the domain registrar (typically the web hosting company or domain name company) replaces your personal contact information with its contact information.

In addition to a website's address, search engines are able to sift through the multitude of websites on the internet to find those suitable to most satisfy whatever term or terms you may have entered in the search bar through a website's META tags. META tags appear in the HEADER section (at the top) of an HTML document and house such information as a brief website's description and keywords.

~

You can find all kinds of websites on the internet. Some are public sites and some are membership sites that you must join in order to access the website content. Some are a combination of both. Of these public or membership sites, the basic types are:

1. Information/Article Sites
2. E-Commerce Sites
3. Gaming Sites
4. Blogs

Information/Article sites provide you with information about a subject, company or individual. E-commerce sites sell products and services. Gaming sites are gambling or other types of game sites. Blogs are a type of information/article site where the owner continually updates and adds posts on a subject often on a daily or weekly basis.

~

Websites can be monetized. By that I mean they can be supplemented with either advertising or products for sale in order to make money for the site owner. Many, many websites are monetized. Commonly, advertising from Google Adsense or affiliate products from Clickbank or Amazon are displayed on the website to help pay for website maintenance costs.

~

Along with the many reputable websites on the internet you can find just as many spam websites. A spam website is usually an anonymous website designed to somehow take your money or make money in some other illegitimate way. However, there are simple things you can do with your website to make sure it is not construed as a spam website by the search engines. Here are some of the basic aspects of a generally "good" website:

1. The content is unique.
2. The Main Content is authoritative, easy to navigate and begins 'above the fold' (the user does not have to scroll the page to reach the beginning of the main

content and at least begins on the 'index' page).

3. The main content is search engine friendly and keyword rich (Keyword RICH not overly SATURATED).

4. The website has provisions for users to users to rate/comment on their opinion quality of the site and how much the site satisfied their intent for visiting the site in the first place.

5. Ad placement is non-obtrusive. The user is not tricked or deceived in any way to click on advertisements and advertisements do not obstruct the main content.

6. The website has an "About" page, describing the authority of the site creator and the purpose of the site.

7. The website has a "Contact" page, denoting where the user can contact the website owner.

8. The website is maintained, keeping content fresh as new information becomes available.

~

Computer programming is very structured and this follows for website programming as well. It is very organized. One way to think of a website's structure is that it is simply a one, two or three column (sometimes more) table that consists of sub-tables and elements. That is exactly how I program my webpages: One main, underlying table with sub-tables and elements. It is also a very simple way to accomplish the website feat.

The underlying table spans all or a portion of the computer screen when is viewed. The span is measured in PIXELS (px for short) and most of my underlying tables span no more than 1500px or they are usually too large for such as a laptop computer's screen. When the website is too large scroll bars appear, making site navigation and viewing clumsy. Most commonly, my underlying tables are 900px or 1200px, depending on the number of columns. If I use a 3 column structure, I may define the table as being 1500px. Typically, I only use a 2 column structure. A 1 column structure could be 900px.

The structuring table houses the main, center section of the website (900px) with either a smaller (up to 300px) column on the left or a smaller (up to 300px) column on the right, or both. The smaller columns contain advertising, perhaps menu navigation buttons or other website elements that are not part of the main content of the website.

Above is a screenshot of the contact page of Denizen-House Enterprises website. See the 2 column table underlying the website structure? The flower-bordered main content of the site is the 900px column with a smaller right column that holds the site's advertising.

Below is a screenshot of an e-commerce website developed by Patti Markow of Denizen-House Enterprises for a third party. Can you recognize the 2 column table underlying this website structure? There is a left column that houses the website navigation menu and advertising while the larger column (900px) the holds the website's main content.

Above is a screenshot of the contact page of another Denizen-House property. This is a 3 column structure. There is a left column which houses the website advertising, a main content center column (larger - 900px) and a right column which houses the site navigation menu.

~

Like the HTML documents are very organized in tables, the website files that contain the documents and other program code are also very organized. A simple website has the following basic files within it's domain directory:

1. Top.php
2. Bottom.php
3. Index.php
4. About.php
5. Contact.php
6. Config.php
7. Style.php

The top.php file declares the HTML document, contains the META tags (header section of the document) and the opening definition of the structural ("body") table. Also in the top.php file is the content of the left column, if any. The bottom.php file contains the content of the right column, if any, the closing definition of the structural ("body") table and the closing HTML document tags. The index.php file contains the content of the main page of the website (the first page visitors view when they are directed via your website's URL). The about.php and contact.php hold the content for the "About" and "Contact" pages. The config.php is the configuration file that hold the definitions of variables that are used throughout the website's pages. The style.php is the CSS (cascading style sheet) for the website that hold style definitions for different website elements.

You will notice that I use .php extensions on all of my website files (with an occasional exception) instead of .html or .htm. The reason for this is that I commonly use at least a little PHP code in the building of my websites and call PHP variables throughout my HTML code. If you use just .html or .htm extension, PHP code and variables will not work even if you code them in.

Lecture 3 - Your Web Host

I intended that these lecture be interactive, so if you are able to get to your computer now please go onto the internet and navigate yourself to the Custom Code Cash online course "Getting Started Page":

http://www.customcodecash.com/started.php

As mentioned earlier, in order for a website to become available to others on the internet, it must be hosted on an internet server. For that you need a web hosting company. The company I recommend is Web Free Hosting and you can find the link to their website appearing as a pink navigation button on the right hand side of the CCC "Getting Started" page.

Web Free Hosting is a VERY reasonably priced web hosting service compared to all of the others out there and their service is EXCELLENT. You will notice that in addition to premium (paid) hosting service, they also have a FREE service. The FREE service is limited, so just like in the online course, I recommend you sign up for a PREMIUM or BUSINESS account. However, for the purpose of just "playing around," you can sign up for the FREE or BASIC account and upgrade later.

[Note: With a FREE account I do not believe you will be able to upload and extract the website files from the website files temple provided with the CCC online course, which means you will have to type all of the coding from scratch. If you want to save yourself A LOT of typing work, I suggest you open at least a BASIC account to start.]

Once you have opened your hosting account and log in, you are brought to your DASHBOARD. It looks like this:

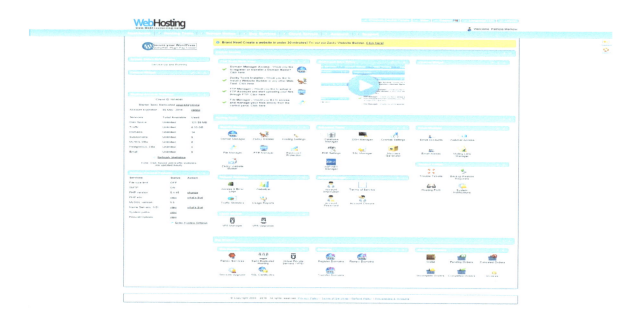

Also as mentioned earlier, in order for a website to be navigated to on the internet, it needs a unique address, or URL. Since, at this point, you are probably only wanting to practice, we will not search for and register what is called a TOP LEVEL DOMAIN. We will use a FREE SUB-DOMAIN which Web Free Hosting makes available. So, your first stop in your hosting account will be to the DOMAIN MANAGER. Click the icon on your dashboard and you will be directed there.

The DOMAIN MANAGER looks like this:

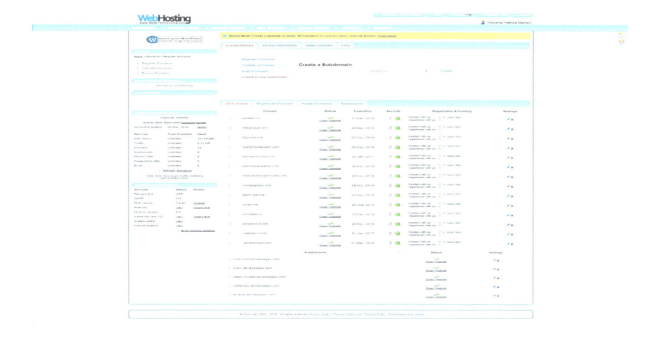

You want to click on: "Creat a Free Subdomain."

A sub-domain is not accessed through www. A sub-domain address looks something like this:

http://subname.atwebpages.com

Select a name for your sub-domain. It can be any name. If the name is already taken, the hosting company will inform you when you click "Create." You also must indicate what the hosting company refers to a "utility domain." These are top level domains that the hosting company owns and permits users to create sub-domains from. I typically use "atwebpages.com".

CREATE YOUR SUB-DOMAIN.

Once you have successfully created a sub-domain, the root directory for the website files will be automatically created in your FILE MANAGER. You can return to your DASHBOARD now and navigate to the FILE MANAGER.

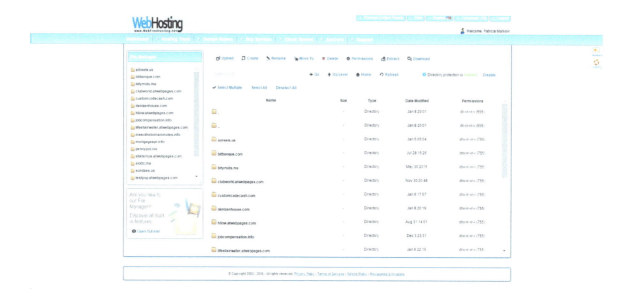

First, you will see a listing of all of your root directories. The root directory of your sub-domain should be there. In an upper right hand corner of the page you will see that "Directory Protection" is ENABLED. DO NOT disable this as you could accidentally delete your root directory and all of your work will be lost.

Now, if you have a least a BASIC hosting account, return to the CCC online course and navigate to the "Course Home" page.   Scroll down the page until you see the ".zip Download" pink link button.

DOWNLOAD THE .ZIP FILE TO YOUR COMPUTER.

DOUBLE-CLICK on the root directory of your sub-domain. There should appear an error page and an index.html page that were automatically created when you created the sub-domain.

On your computer you should now have a "website.zip" folder. You are going to upload it into this sub-directory (where the error and index html pages appear). Click the "Upload" button on the top of the page then click "click to select files."

Select the "website.zip" folder from your computer a click "Upload."

A .zip folder is a SEALED folder that can be manipulated like a file (such as for a file upload). However, because it is sealed, the server cannot access the files inside of the folder. You have to EXTRACT them.

One of the buttons on the top of your FILE MANAGER page read: "Extract".
SELECT the website.zip folder by clicking on it ONCE. Then click "Extract."
The FILE MANAGER will ask you to confirm that you want to extract the .zip
folder. Confirm that you do.

When the file extraction is complete, you will see that an OPEN folder called
"website" was created. This is a sub-directory of your domain root directory and
houses your future website's folders and files. What you need to do now is
POINT your domain to the sub-directory called WEBSITE.

Return to your DASHBOARD and navigate once again to the DOMAIN
MANAGER. The bottom half of the DOMAIN MANAGER lists all of the
domains and sub-domains of your hosting account. Locate your sub-domain.

In the domain list table there is a column called: "Setting" that contains what
appears to be a tool icon. Click on the tool icon for your sub-domain.

When you click on it you will see the headings of the tools table. The first column
reads: "Pointers"; the next column reads: "DNS"; the third column reads: "Delete
Subdomain".

Click on the column that reads POINTERS.

You are going to KEEP the selection of "Hosting Path Local". You will also see
an input box that is for the HOSTING PATH. It will already read the path of your
subdomain, you just have to add the path to your sub-directory "website". AT
THE END of the path as it already appears, type: "/website" (without the quotes).
Then click "Save Path".

Your domain has been REDIRECTED to your sub-directory WEBSITE. At this
point, if you type the URL of your sub-domain into the address bar of your
browser (in a new tab, of course), the website template should appear and you
have the beginnings of your new website already done for you. If not, you will
have to CREATE the basic files in the directory of your domain and type the
coding yourself. There are also 2 FOLDERS you should create within your root

directory: FONTS and IMAGES. In the FONTS sub-folder you will upload your special font files. In the IMAGES sub-folder you will upload all of the images for your website. These folders are already included in the website template from the CCC online course.

Lecture 4 - Creating Files and Folders

From your web hosting account DASHBOARD, navigate to the FILE MANAGER if you are not already there. DOUBLE-CLICK on the ROOT DIRECTORY for you sub-domain. You should have, at least, the ERROR page and the INDEX.HTML page. If you participated using the CCC online course with at least a BASIC hosting account, you should also have the website.zip file and the website folder.

For those with the open website folder (the website sub-directory), you should DOUBLE-CLICK on the open website folder to be in the correct directory for creating additional files and folders.

~

Creating files and folders for your website is extremely easy.

At the top of the FILE MANAGER, and within your proper DIRECTORY or SUB-DIRECTORY, you will see a button called: "Create". To create a file or folder for you website, click on it.

From the pop-up that appears, you can choose to create either a folder or a file. Most often, you will be creating files. All you have to do is select the option you need, name it and click "Create".

To name a folder, you do not use a name extension such as .php or .html. However, to name a file you MUST have an extension. I use .php for the naming of all of my files, with rare exception when I occasionally use .htm or .html. ALSO, be sure your new folder or file names are unique. You do not want to name a file or folder with the same name as a file or folder that already exists.

IF YOU ARE NOT USING THE CCC ONLINE COURSE WEBSITE TEMPLATES, create your folders and files now.

FOLDERS: fonts
            images

FILES: config.php
      style.php
      top.php
      bottom.php
      index.php
      about.php
      contact.php

Lecture 5 - Website Coding Overview

Website coding should be very organized and well documented. In a way, the coding itself is kept organized by the simple requirements of its syntax. However, in addition to the syntax, you should document your script by inserting comments within the code. Website coding should also be done LOGICALLY. THINK what you want to accomplish with the code, then STEP BY STEP code the commands necessary to achieve your purpose.

~

I think of website coding syntax as being either VERTICAL or HORIZONTAL. I consider the opening and closing tags of code sections to be VERTICAL. I consider the opening and closing tags of ELEMENTS to be HORIZONTAL.

HTML documents have VERTICAL opening and closing tags such as <html>...</html>, <header>....</header>, <body>....</body>. HTML elements have HORIZONTAL tags that define the ELEMENT within the HTML document, such as <p>...</p> (paragraph), <table>...</table> (table).

PHP (which is an acronym for "PHP: Hypertext Preprocessor") has VERTICAL tags, indicating a PHP section of code: <?php .... ?>.

JAVASCRIPT has the opening tag of <script> and the closing tag of </script>. CSS (style) has the opening tag of <style> and the closing tag of </style>.

Commenting in PHP and JAVASCRIPT has an opening of /* and a closing of */. Commenting in HTML has an opening of <!- - and a closing of - ->.

Lecture 6 - config.php File

The config.php file is your website configuration file. It houses PHP variables that will be utilized throughout the coding of your website and, in the future, the hosting information for your Mysql database.

[The website template from the CCC online course is geared toward the creation of an information/article website. Later, you can always modify or expand the code to create any kind of website you desire. However, for your first website, I recommend you do a simple information/article website.]

Within the website template, I have defined variables that are relative to the overall website. The code looks like this:

(config.php)

```php
<?php

/* Site URL */

$url="http://sitetemps.atwebpages.com";

/* Display URL (without 'http://') */

$displayurl="DisplayUrl.com";

/* Site Name */

$sitename="Site Name";

/* Site Colors */

$backgroundcolor="black";
$sitecolor="pink";
$bordercolor="hotpink";
```

```
/* Navigation/Page Name Buttons */

$page1nav="Home";
$page2nav="Page 2 Name";
$page3nav="Page 3 Name";
$page4nav="About";
$page5nav="Contact";

/* Images example: imagename.png */

$favimage=" ";
$facebookimage=" ";
$page1image=" ";
$page2image=" ";
$page3image=" ";
$aboutimage="pattibw.jpg";
$contactimage="email.png";




?>
```

[Note: The website template from CCC online course also provides for 2 additional pages in order to create a 3 article, 5 page site. If you are not using the template, feel free to create 2 additionals .php page files: page2.php and page3.php.]

The first and most important variable in the config.php file is the $url variable, which is the URL of your website. If you forget to configure this, it could effect the entire working of your website.

If you are using the CCC online course website template, remember you have already set the path pointing to the subdirectory in the domain manager, so you do not have to add the pointing in your URL (that would look something like this: http://sitetemps.atwebpages.com/website).

Take a look at the other variables I have set within the config.php file. They are basically self-explanatory.

IMPORTANT: After you make changes to any file, BE SURE TO CLICK "SAVE" at the bottom of the file page.

TYPE YOUR WEBSITE URL BETWEEN THE QUOTES OF THE $url VARIABLE in the config.php file NOW.

CLICK "SAVE".

Entering your website URL is all you have to imminently do. I will go through the other website files first, to give the non-template users a chance to type all the coding while at the same time explaining the code as it appears to those of you who are using the template. Non-template users can type the code exactly as it appears with the exception of the URL. Enter your website URL sub-domain and remember to click enter both at various times while you are typing the coding and when you have finished.

[Note: To get inside of a website file, where you type the coding, DOUBLE-CLICK on the file name in the directory or sub-directory.]

Lecture 7 - style.php File

The style.php file is your website cascading style sheet. A cascading style sheet often has the extension of .css, but I commonly call PHP variables within my style sheet so I use the extension of .php.

Within the style sheet you can pre-define styles for different HTML elements that you will use on your website. You can also code IN-LINE style, which I also do for style that is to be associated with only one element and not more than one. IN-LINE styling is done using the "style=" command within the elements opening tag. Style sheet styling is more for overall styling or styling that will be called more than once for more than one element. Using the style sheet saves having to re-type the styling over and over as would have to be done with IN-LINE styling, every time you want to use a particular style.

The coding for a basic style sheet that is included with the template looks like this:

(style.php)
```php
<?php


?>
<style>

body {

 background: url() no-repeat center center fixed;
          -webkit-background-size: cover;
          -moz-background-size: cover;
          -o-background-size: cover;
          background-size: cover;
          background-size: 100% 100%;
          background: <?php echo $backgroundcolor ?>;
color: black;

}
```

```css
a:link {text-decoration: none;color:hotpink}
a:hover {color:white}
a:visited {color:red}



@font-face {
   font-family: firstfont;

          src: url(fonts/kley.otf);

}

@font-face {
font-family: secondfont;
src: url(fonts/Precious.ttf);
src: url(fonts/Precious.woff);

}

@font-face {
font-family: thirdfont;
src: url(fonts/actionj.ttf);

}
    #fontz {
         font-family: firstfont;
    }
    #fontz2 {
    font-family: secondfont;
    }
    #fontz3 {
    font-family: thirdfont;
    }
```

```
#butt {
border: groove 7px <?php echo $bordercolor ?>;
border-radius: 50px;
background: <?php echo $sitecolor ?>;
font-weight: bold;
font-size: 18px;
height: 35px;
width: 150px;
float: left;
color: black;
margin-top: .35em;
margin-bottom: .35em;
margin-right: .25em;
}
```

</style>

For those that are not using the template, they can type the code exactly as it appears above. Non-template users do not have the special font faces that come with the template, so the sections that refer to FONT ('@font-face','#fontz','#fontz2',' #fontz3') can be left out.

As we are building the website, we will be returning to the config.php file and the style.php file for updating/modifying the code. What the code means will be discussed at that time. Much if it is self-explanatory. For now, just look through the code and write down what questions you may have. If your questions are not answered in a later lecture, shoot me an email. I plan to release future editions of these lectures with a "Frequently Asked Questions" (FAQs) Section, so don't be afraid to email me no matter what your questions might be.

denizenhouse@gmail.com

Lecture 8 - top.php File

The top.php file is a file that will be called and included in the coding of every page of your website. It houses the document declaration, the header section and META tags, the opening HTML <body> tag, the opening definitions of the overall website structure table and the navigation menu.

The top.php file is more complex than the config.php and style.php files, so I will go through it a section at a time in an effort to avoid confusion.

~

First, we have the HTML document declaration:

```
<!-- Document Declaration -->

<!DOCTYPE html>
```

Immediately following, we insert a PHP code section that calls/includes the config.php and style.php files:

```
<!-- PHP file includes -->

<?php
include "config.php";
include "style.php";

?>
```

After the "includes," we have the opening HTML tag:

```
<!-- HTML Declaration -->

<html xmlns="http://www.w3.org/1999/xhtml" >
```

Once we have opened HTML, we code in the HEADER section which includes the META tags:

```
<!-- Header -->

<head>

<!-- Favicon -->

<link rel="shortcut icon" href="<?php echo $url ?>/images/<?php echo $favimage ?>" type="image/png">

<!-- Site Title -->

<title><?php echo $sitename ?></title>

<!-- Meta Tags -->

    <meta http-equiv="Content-Type" content="text/html; charset=utf-8">
    <meta name="description" content="<!-- enter site description -->">
    <meta name="keywords" content="<!-- enter comma separated keywords/keyword phrases -->">

    <META property="og:image" content="<?php echo $url ?>/images/<?php echo $facebookimage ?>">
    <META property="og:url" content="<?php echo $url ?>">
    <META property="og:type" content="website">
    <META property="og:title" content="<?php echo $sitename ?>">
    <META property="og:description" content="<!-- copy & paste site description from above -->">


</head>
```

We put the opening HEAD tag first, to open the code section.

Next, we define the FAVICON. The FAVICON is that tiny image that appears with your website's name in the browser tab when the website is navigated to.

After the FAVICON, we define the site title. This is the site name as is will appear with the FAVICON in the browser tab when a visitor is on the site.

Next come the META tags. As you recall, the META tags are used by the search engines to help them distinguish your website from others when searching for websites that will satisfy a user's intent after they enter a keyword or search term in the search engine's search bar. You have to remove the comments and add the site's description and keywords on each site individually. I do not call PHP variables (defined in the config.php file) like I do in other sections of the top.php file. The Open Graph META tags (META property="og:...") are used by facebook when someone "likes" or "shares" your website.

Following the META tags is the closing HEADER tag (</head>).

The HEADER section of the HTML document is now done. Now, we can begin defining the document BODY by coding the opening BODY tag (<body>). Like the opening HTML tag (<html....>), the CLOSING tag will be included in the bottom.php file.

```
<!-- Document Body -->

 <body>
```

In this day and age, I assumed that all of you will want to have your website equipped with a Facebook "like" button. In which case, I included in the template the coding required for placement immediately after the opening BODY tag in order for the Facebook button to work. Note that it is JAVASCRIPT (as can be detected by the opening (<script>) and closing (</script>) JAVASCRIPT tags:

```
<!-- Facebook Required Script -->

    <div id="fb-root"></div>
<script>(function(d, s, id) {
  var js, fjs = d.getElementsByTagName(s)[0];
  if (d.getElementById(id)) return;
  js = d.createElement(s); js.id = id;
  js.src = "//connect.facebook.net/en_US/all.js#xfbml=1";
  fjs.parentNode.insertBefore(js, fjs);
}(document, 'script', 'facebook-jssdk'));</script>
```

Now we can start to define the structural table for our website. We start with the root table:

```
<!-- Overall Site Definition Table -->

<center><table width="1100"><tr>
```

Note that I defined the overall site to be "centered" (<center>) in the browser window and the overall site to be 1100px in width. This coding constitutes the OPENING table declaration. The CLOSING of this table will be coded in the bottom.php file.

<tr> means "table row". The site definition table will only have 1 row (so I coded it with the opening table declaration) with 1 to 3 columns. The closing </tr> tag will also be coded in the bottom.php file.

Within our structural table we have 2 columns (in the template). The left column is the wider column that will house the main site content. A column in a table is declared with opening <td> and closing </td> tags. So, working left to right, the declaration of our main content section of our site comes next:

```
<!-- Main Site Definition Table -->

<td>

<center><table width="900"><tr><td bgcolor=<?php echo $sitecolor ?> style="border-radius:
25px">
        <div style="border: groove 35px <?php echo $bordercolor ?>;border-radius:
25px">


                <table width="900">


    <tr><td>
```

The column for the main content is 900px wide. Note the "style=" code where I apply some IN-LINE styling. In this case, the rounded corners of the site with the "border-radius: 25px" code.

Then I coded in an HTML division (<div...) in order to add some additional IN-LINE styling. In this case, the border style "groove" to be 35px wide in a color defined in our config.php file.

The next embedded table (within the overall structural table) is the table that defines the website header. The website header is the banner-like section that appears at the top of every page of the website:

```
<!-- Header Table -->

        <center><table style="border: groove 10px <?php echo $bordercolor ?>"
cellpadding="0" cellspacing="0">
<tr>

    <td width="900" height="125" valign="center">
        <center><table width="900"><tr><td>

        <b><font size=5 id="fontz">  Site Lead-In</font></b>           <center>
        <font size=7 style="text-shadow: 5px 5px 5px <?php echo $bordercolor ?>; font-family:
'verdana'"><b> Site Subject</b>
    </font></center>
        </td></tr></table></center>
```
```
        </td>
```
```
    </tr>
        </table></center></td></tr></table>
```

I coded in a "Site Lead-In" the code of which can be eliminated if you do not want a site lead-in. The "Site Subject" is basically the title of your site. Note a few HTML tags that I used:

<b> ... </b> - The characters inbetween the "b" tags will be font-weight BOLD.
<font>... </font> - The characters inbetween the "font" tags will have the style defined within the opening tag. I use "font size" and the style of "text-shadow" and I also define a "font-family". " " is the HTML coding for a "space".

The next embedded table is the one that will hold our DISPLAY URL (which we will or have specified in the $displayurl PHP variable in our config.php file). The display URL is WITHOUT the http:// preamble. It is always a good idea for your website to reiterate it's URL in it's header so that the visitor can easily see (and better remember) the website he is visiting.

The code looks like this:

```
<!-- Display URL Table -->

<center><table width="900"><tr><td bgcolor=<?php echo $bordercolor ?>>
        <center><font size=4 color=#000000><b><?php echo $displayurl
?></b></font></center>
        </td></tr></table></center>
```

Lastly in our top.php file we have the coding for the embedded table that will house our website navigation buttons/menu. Later in the lectures we will discuss how to place the navigation menu either in a left or right column and/or only have the navigation menu appear on certain pages. But for now, we'll set the navigation menu just above the main content and to appear on all of our pages.

I also like to use buttons as opposed to just text links for my website navigation. The STYLE for the buttons is in the style.php file with the identity of "#butt". The "#" indicates that the STYLE will be called with the "id=" command somewhere within the opening HTML element tag. In this case, I am calling the style within an <input ...> tag associated with a link (<a>...</a>). An <input...> tag does not have a CLOSING tag (/input). A link tag DOES have a closing tag (</a>).

Another note is that I made the BACKGROUND for the display URL table the color black, denoted by the "bgcolor="#000000". Alternatively, this could have been coded: style="background: black". "#000000" is simply the HEX notation for the color black. Since black is a recognized color name, the word "black" can also be used.

The site navigation menu/button table code is as follows:

```html
<!-- Site Navigation Button Table -->


<center><table border="0" cellspacing="0" cellpadding="0" width="900" >
                <tr><td align="center" bgcolor="#000000">
                <div style="margin-left: 65px">
<a href="<?php echo $url ?>/index.php" ><input type="button" id="butt" value="<?php echo
$page1nav ?>"></a>
     <a href="<?php echo $url ?>/page2.php"><input type="button" id="butt" value="<?php
echo $page2nav ?>"></a>

     <a href="<?php echo $url ?>/page3.php"><input type="button" id="butt" value="<?php
echo $page3nav ?>"></a>
     <a href="<?php echo $url ?>/about.php"><input type="button" id="butt" value="<?php
echo $page4nav ?>"></a>
     <a href="<?php echo $url ?>/contact.php"><input type="button" id="butt" value="<?php
echo $page5nav ?>"></a>
     </div>
                </td></tr></table></center>
```

REMEMBER TO CLICK "SAVE" AFTER YOU CODE OR MODIFY CODE
WITHIN YOUR WEBSITE FILES.

Lecture 9 - bottom.php File

The bottom.php file, like the top.php file, will be called and included with the code of every one of your website pages. It contains the copyright declaration, the code for the right column, if any, the closing tags for the main structural table and the </body> and </html> closing tags.

First, code in the FOOTER (the copyright declaration):

```
<br>

<br>
<center><table style="BACKGROUND-COLOR:#000000" width="900">
<tr><td>
<center><font size=4 color=<?php echo $sitecolor ?>><b>Copyright <?php echo date(Y)." "
?> - Your Name - All Rights Reserved</b></font></center>
     </td></tr></table></center>
```


 (with no required closing tag) codes in a blank line.

Then code in the closing tags for the main content COLUMN of the structural table (the wider, left [in this case] column - 900px):

```
<br>
</div>
</td>
</tr></table></center>
</td>
```

After closing the main content column (left column) within our website structure, we can OPEN the code for our right column - the one that, in this case, holds the code for our website's advertising:

```
<td valign="top">
<br><br>
<center>
<!-- Paste adsense 120 x 240 ad zone code here -->
```

You can paste in up to 3 ad zones, separated by a blank line (<br>). 3 ad zones is typically the maximum number of ad zones that can be shown on a page per advertising network. In this case, I use Google Adsense. However, any advertising network can be used.

Lastly, CLOSE out the right column AND the entire HTML document with the following code:

```
</td></tr></table></center>
</body>
</html>
```

Lecture 10 - index.php File - Part 1

Thus far, you have seen and/or coded (if you are not using the CCC template) the config.php, style.php, top.php and bottom.php files. At this point we can put it together so that you can see what has been already completed.

We will start with the index.php file.

Every website MUST have an index file. It can be .html or .php, but it must be named "index". The index file is the home page of a website and is automatically available to viewing as soon as a visitor navigates to the website. At the absolute minimal, it is possible to have a website where the only file and page is the index.

For those of you who are not using the template, you can view what you have coded so far by adding some "includes" in your index file. To access where you should put the code (open the file), double-click on the index.php file in your directory. You should see a blank page.

Simply type in the following "includes":

```
<?php
include "top.php";
?>




<?php
include "bottom.php";
?>
```

Now, when you navigate to your sub-domain (type the URL into the address bar of the browser) you will see the beginnings of your website.

We will go further into coding the index.php file after the next lecture.

Lecture 11 - Penning Profits

As stated earlier, the type of website we will be first putting together interactively between these lectures and the Custom Code Cash online course is an information/article website. And an aspect of a "good" website is unique content.

Before we go any further with the development of the website itself, it is time to put together your content. There are services that will create unique content for you - at a price. You can find the information on how to put together pieces of unique content using services in the online course. But I have found that, in addition to website coding, writing unique, search engine optimized articles myself is also satisfying and fun. It's also a little challenging, if you like a challenge.

Why write?

When all is said and done, one must realize a particular fact that will always remain true: The overwhelming majority of people who use the internet are in search of information, not necessarily for something to buy. From this comes the saying that anyone who gets involved with moneymaking online is familiar with:

CONTENT IS KING!

What is content? Content is all of the words on the internet, largely in the form of articles and the information made available on websites. There are approximately 25 billion or more pages of content currently indexed on the web. Someone had to write all of that content and, regardless of the amazing number of written pieces of work that are already existent, there will always be a demand for more. Sure, there is a lot of SPAM, such as a single article appearing exactly the same in many directories and on many sites, but godfather Google has been able to manage this by making these articles more or less obscure to an internet search user. Getting banned by Google is something you want to avoid.

The demand is for innovative, unique work and the opportunity to publish such work is freely open to everyone. One need not even wrack their brain in order to write something that has never been written before. An author can research a subject on the internet and simply combine, in their own words, the information found on multiple sites. Then an innovative and new approach to that information can be incorporated into the work, making exactly the kind of written piece that Google, and the web searching public, should love. Such work, called "unique content," can be monetized, becoming a source of potential and sometimes substantial income for the author.

An author of unique content does not have to publish his work in his own name. There are numerous sites on the internet that hire writers who will ultimately be selling their rights to their work to others. Those others usually publish the work in their own name and monetize it with advertising and the sale of products and services. However, the original author usually ends up working for a mere pittance. Between the research, writing and the "cut" the broker site takes, an author can only make a one-time fee that typically equates to somewhere between $1 and $5 per hour. It is potentially more profitable for an author to publish and monetize his work himself, as Custom Code Cash teaches. Through this method, there can be residual, passive income produced for the author for many years to come. Alternatively, by publishing the unique, search engine optimized content on a custom coded website, the content can be sold at a much increased profit. This produces lump-sum, one-time income when needed.

What to write about?

You can literally write about anything, but it is recommended that you steer clear of subjects that are of an illegal or are otherwise offensive nature. What is recommended by almost all experts is that the subject of the web content one creates should be considered "evergreen" in order to be most successful. Evergreen subjects are subjects that have already stood the test of time. They are popular, the most searched for and, in all likelihood, will continue to be of interest to internet users for years and years to come.

There are three main niches that are truly evergreen:

1) Health and Fitness/Weight Loss
2) Love and Relationships/Dating
3) Personal Finance/How to Make Money/Make Money Online

If an author writes about anything related to the above niches, his work will not become outdated as quickly as fad subjects or news stories. Hence, the word "evergreen" is used to described such content.

There are a lot of sub-niches that can be thought of that are still related to the main evergreen niches, such as "The use of fruit to make home-made beauty treatments,""How to qualify for a home mortgage" and "Birthday present ideas for a boyfriend." From these examples, one can see that there are many, many possibilities when it comes to finding something to write about.

Occasionally, a writer will run into a "writer's block" and seem to be stymied when trying to think of a subject. There are several websites that offer assistance to writers who are in search of article ideas. One site is the Google Adwords Keyword tool. An author can simply type a general subject into the search term box and run a search of all of the related keywords. Examination of the resultant keywords can trigger ideas. If there are subjects of interest in the list of keywords that are returned, an author can do another search, and continue searching, by typing the subject(s) of interest into the search term box and running the tool.

Another site that offers title ideas to authors is exinearticles.com. In order to take advantage of the title suggestion tool, one needs to sign up as an ezinearticles author. There is no charge for this. Once logged into his account, an author can click on the writing and editing tab. After navigating to the writing and editing platform of the website, in the left-hand column of the page one will see a link to proceed to the title suggestion tool. Possible titles can be searched by category and keywords. The titles suggested by the tool are, to the best of knowledge, subjects that ezinearticles authors have yet to write about. So it would be worthwhile to consider these titles for use on a new work.

"How to" articles are usually well received and are popular on the internet. For suggestions of "how to"s that an author can pen there is a site called wikihow.com. At the wikihow site there is a "how to" subject suggestion tool that anyone can use. No account is necessary. An author can search for subjects by category or even elect to utilize the random feature, where a random "how to" will be returned when the author clicks "surprise me."

A unique content project can consist of one or more articles. For the sake of our information website - at least our first one - we will say that a complete project is made up of three related articles.

* Lead Article
* 2 Supporting Articles

The objective of the lead article is to drive organic (search engine) traffic. It will target a primary keyword that offers the opportunity for the article to rank in a preferred search result position and receive the most traffic when published on the custom coded information website. The lead article should appear on the "home"/"index" page of the website and will be the first article to be viewed by a visitor when they navigate to the site. The lead article should be optimized for the "rankable/traffic" primary keyword and could also contain a YouTube video. The lead article will be linked, via the website navigation buttons, to the two supporting articles.

When an internet user types a word or phrase into the search box, there can be millions of related web pages that result. These pages are called "SERP"s (Search Engine Result Pages). A preferred ranking position would be one of the ten possible listings that appear on the first search result page.

The two supporting articles should be written on subjects that are related to the lead article and their objective is to maximize income. They will target primary, high-cost keywords, according to Google Adwords. By high-cost it is meant that advertisers are paying the most money to target their advertisements to those particular keywords. The Google Adwords keyword tool will supply the information necessary for the selection of the primary keywords for the supporting articles.

In the Custom Code Cash online course, I present a rather quick method that I use to find primary and LSI (Latent Search Indexing) keywords. You will find the link to that part of the course on the "Course Home" page and then scroll down to the "preliminaries" where "keywords" is listed.

What is Search Engine Optimization?

One of the goals of a web content creator is to have his content rank in one of the top ten positions on the first page of search engine search results. In order to achieve this goal, content must be search engine optimized. Primarily, search engine optimization is done through the strategic use of keywords within the content. High search engine rankings can also be achieved through links back to the content page that are featured on other related web pages, called "backlinks."

For the purpose of these lectures, search engine optimization does not have to be made into a major, complex project in itself. Writing keyword-rich content and including the primary keyword in the article title, along with inclusion in at least one sub-heading, is basically all that is necessary. Embedding a video on the same page as the lead article also creates a high quality link for the article, working toward the creator's SEO advantage.

Use of LSI (Latent Search Indexed or "secondary") Keywords:

One of the potential problems a content creator may stumble upon is keyword spamming. Remember, a "good" website is keyword RICH, not overly SATURATED. Although a primary keyword should be used to a specific density, over use of the primary keyword can work in a detrimental fashion, causing the content to be less worthy of ranking by Google. To avoid this potential dilemma, yet in order to emphasize the key subject of the content, LSI, or "secondary," keywords are used. LSI keywords are not used in place of the primary keyword, they are used in addition to.

To find the related LSI keywords for any primary keyword, one need return to the Google Adwords keyword tool. In the search term box, type the primary keyword EXACTLY. Be sure "exact match" is selected for the match type and have the results sorted by relevancy. The resultant keyword list contains all LSI keywords. One should select up to 10 LSI keywords for any given primary keyword. The criteria is only that the LSI keyword be able to be incorporated easily into the article being written. Not all 10 of the LSI keywords need to be used. But at least five LSI keywords should be used for an article with a length of 500 words. For a 1000 word article, you should probably strive to use all 10.

For the purpose of keyword organization and reference while composing the 3 articles of content for the website, do the following:

* Make 3 separate keyword lists
* At the top of each list, write one of the primary keywords for the 3 articles
* Skip a line and write the 2 other primary keywords for the related articles
* Skip another line and write a list of the 10 LSI keywords that can be included in the content.

Long-Tail Keywords:

A long-tail keyword is a keyword phrase that contains four, five or more words. Many internet entrepreneurs have touted tremendous success using long-tails instead of the standard keywords provided by the Google Keyword Research Tool. One of the primary benefits of using a long-tail keyword is that it will be easier to rank on the first page of the search results. There is also a down site to long-tails. Traffic can be dramatically lower than the use of standard keywords and Google does not maintain nor provide information, such as monthly searches, competition and estimated CPC, in its database. In effect, the long-tail user is basically using the keyword blind.

The suggestion here is to use long-tail keywords as primary keywords only in the event that standard keywords cannot be found that meet the analyzed, filtered criteria that is being used. For example, after analysis of many keywords and there is no keyword that is found where competing pages have page ranks less than two, then perhaps one should consider using a long-tail keyword as the primary keyword.

You can learn the page rankings of competing sites for your keyword using the "seoquake" toolbar extension available from Google. It is free.

Too find a long-tail keyword, one need only type "how to" or "why" or something similar in front of the best primary keyword in the Google search bar. As one is typing, he will notice the Google auto-suggest feature is recommending additional words to complete the phrase. That phrase that is being auto-suggested is a long-tail keyword that people have actually searched for, although exactly how many people cannot be determined. By playing with the auto-suggest feature, a suitable long-tail keyword will most likely be able to be found. The auto-suggest feature is also another way to get suggestions for possible titles to articles.

Equipped with the subjects and keywords for your lead and supporting articles, it's time to sit down and get to work on composition.

Basic Article Format:

A basic, QUALITY article has three primary components:

* Introduction
* Body Paragraphs
* Conclusion

In the introduction, the article subject is defined and something along the lines of a hypothesis, premise, approach or objective that the author will meet within the article is stated. The body paragraphs, usually not less than three, logically present the facts that support the hypothesis, premise, approach or objective presented in the introduction. The conclusion simply repeats everything that the reader has been told in the article, summarized, of course, and makes a final statement as to how the hypothesis, premise, approach or objective was proven.

As a writer becomes more experienced, he will develop his own style of writing. For example, in some circumstances a concluding paragraph may seem unnecessary and the writer will choose not to write one. Article style can be appropriated to the various subjects and situations that the writer comes across during his writing career.

For the purpose of adding a little style to your writing right from the start, the following features were found to be requested by many individuals and businesses who hire writers to create their content:

* A Bulleted List of List of Points
* Sub-headings

When just beginning to write articles, it is a good practice to start to become accustom to adding a bulleted list or bulleted points. This feature makes an article easier to skim by the reader and generally indicates a better quality, logically presented piece of work.

A bulleted list or points can be placed immediately following the introductory paragraph or elsewhere in the article body, as determined to be appropriate. There should be a minimum of 3 points or 3 items to the list, but on occasion less may only be called for - on occasion, more. The points or list of items presented should logically be followed up by the body paragraphs that immediately follow the bulleted section. The list can also be related to the sub-headings that the author intends to use in his article format.

Usually, an article of approximately 500 words can have a minimum of 3 sub-headings, separating the different sections of the article. There can be less or more, depending on the article length and the manner in which the article author wants to present his case. Sub-headings are also a feature that people who hire writers seem to request quite often and, again, it makes the article easier to skim by the reader and helps with the logical glow of the article's paragraphs. One or more body paragraphs can be written for each sub-heading.

Generally, sentences and paragraphs should be kept as short as necessary to make their point. This makes the article easier to read. Long, complex sentences should be made into multiple shorter sentences. Paragraphs should be composed of between two and five sentences. Multiple paragraphs should be created if the point being made warrants more sentences.

To write a search engine optimized article is not extremely difficult once the writer becomes accustom to writing with keywords. In the beginning, it may be a good idea for the writer to write the article without paying too much attention to the keyword density. After the article is written, the author can go back over the article and insert the necessary keywords in places where they are appropriate, finally insuring that the proper density of the keywords has been met.

The following are general guidelines for keyword placement:

* The primary keyword should be used in the Article Title;
* The primary keyword should be used with a density of between 2% and 4% throughout the entire article;
* The primary keyword should be used in the first sentence of the first paragraph;
* In addition to the first sentence, the primary keyword should be used at least one more time in the first paragraph;

* The primary keyword should be used in at least one sub-heading;
* The primary keyword should appear once or twice in the closing paragraph;
* LSI keywords should have a total density of about 1%.

By keyword density, it is meant that, depending on the length of the article, the keyword should appear as many times as necessary to make the article word composition equal to a certain percentage. For example, for a 500 word article, the primary keyword should appear 10 to 20 times, making the density 2% to 4%. Do not count the use of the keyword in the title. Do count the use of the keyword in the sub-headings.

For LSI keywords, the total density should be about 1%. LSI keywords need be used only once each up to the number amounting to the density percentage. For example, in a 500 word article, total LSI keyword density should be about 1%. That means a total of approximately 5 LSI keywords should be used once each.

Keywords should be worked into the article where they are appropriate and make sense. An article should not just be keyword stuffed where the keyword placement is out of context or affects the readability of the article.

USING A VIDEO TO ENHANCE SEARCH ENGINE OPTIMIZATION:

The use of videos to help an article or website rank in the search results is a technique that has been successful time and time again. Videos are much easier to rank that static website pages. By embedding an optimized video, one that will usually achieve a rank position within 30 minutes of upload, an important link is shared by the video and the static page one wants to rank.

The page rank 9 link (YouTube has a page rank of 9) enhances the optimization of the static page, helping it to achieve a high rank than without the video. In addition, YouTube is the second largest search engine in the world, so the link of the static page in the video description can encourage additional organic traffic.

You can embed a video that is already available on YouTube. Just be sure the ENTIRE video is related to your subject and that the video is not just an advertisement or is overly interfered with by advertising. Preferably, no advertisements should be present at all. You can also create your own video.

One method I used to use to create my own video was to create a powerpoint presentation and then convert it to video. I would add images and music. Creating a good video requires a little time, but the benefit is that you are in charge of the optimization. In the next lecture, I discuss the technique for optimizing a home-made video.

If you opt to create your own video, also a fun sort of challenge, be sure to use only images you are free to use and music that you are free to use. You want to avoid any kind of copyright infringement. In the CCC online course "Getting Started" page are pink link buttons for PIXABAY (where you can get free images that can be used commercially) and for MUSIC4YOURVIDS (where you can get free music that can be used commercially). Also, in closing your video, be sure to give credit to Pixabay and Music4yourvids as the providers of your images and music.

Lecture 12 - Home-Made Video Optimization

If you decide to create your own video, which can be done in any number of ways and far too many ways for me to discuss, there is a technique I have had tremendous success with in the days when I took the time to develop videos. By optimizing your article AND the home-made video that goes along with it, that's twice as much chance you have to be recognized favorably by the search engines.

First, the keyword list for the article you are creating the video for should be handy in order to optimize the vide, targeting the same keywords. The following is a general guideline for video SEO:

* Use the primary keyword in the video title. The video can have the same title as the article.

* In the video description, put the link to your website FIRST.

* Following the link to your website, list the keywords. List the primary keyword first, followed by the LSI keywords on the list. This can be done in paragraph format provided the keywords are comma separated.

* On your computer clipboard, copy the comma separated keyword "paragraph" (without the link to your website).

* Paste the keyword "paragraph" once again further down the description page (an "article" belongs between the 2 keyword "paragraphs").

* Paste the keyword "paragraph" into the "tags" section.

* Write a few paragraphs between the 2 keyword "paragraphs", making use of the primary keyword (use it several times) and the LSI keywords.

* The few paragraphs that are written should be related to the video, perhaps another summary of the your article (but do not use any verbatim sections of the article- it will appear as duplicate content which is frowned upon by Google).

* Select the most appropriate category for the video.

* Select "standard" YouTube license.

* Be sure to save all changes.

* From the "video manager", click on the video to view it.

* "Like" your own video.

* Click on the "share" link. The "embed" code must be copied and ultimated pasted into position on your website page.

Lecture 13 - index.php File - Part Two

For those of you not using the template, thus far with the index page coding we have the "includes." Next, remembering that a "good" website provides for user input/comment/rating, I have found that using a star rater on my information websites works very well.

There is a pink button link that appears on the CCC online course "Getting Started" page for the "Website Star Rater" site. Underneath the code for my "top.php" include, I place the star rater first. On the star rater website, all you have to do is select the rater that your want (3-5 stars and star color) and be sure to match the background color to your website sitecolor.

On the CCC online course "Course Home" page, under "preliminaries" on the right hand side, are the links to the sections of the course that cover "images" and "colors." You can choose to cover those sections now, or simply insert your star rater after you cover the images and color sections of the course.

For the insertion of the star rater is the following code:

```
<center><small><b>Please take a Moment and Rate this Site:</b></small><br>

<!-- Replace the following star rating code and paste your own star rating code here: -->

</center>
<br>
```

Next on the index page, which is generally the same as will be on the subsequent article pages, is the code to define the embedded table that makes up the page. It is 2 column, with a border divider between the columns.

The following code opens the main embedded table and defines the first (wide, article) column:

```
<center><table width="900"><tr>
```

```
<td width="650" valign="top">
<div style="margin-left: 15px;margin-right: 15px">

<!-- Page 1 Article -->

<center><h1> Article Title</h1></center>

<p> Introductory Paragraph</p>

<h2> Subheader 1</h2>

<p>Paragraph</p>

<h2> Subheader 2</h2>

<p> Paragraph</p>

<h2> Subheader 3</h2>

<p> Paragraph</p>

<p> Closing Paragraph</p>

<br>
</div>
</td>
```

Note the DIVISION <div...> that is defined to set the STYLE for the left and right margins. You can see where you can copy and paste the sections of your article. <h1>...<h2> are HEADING tags. <p> is a PARAGRAPH tag.

You may want to insert a little dividing line between the paragraph(s) under your last sub-heading in order to separate if from your concluding/closing paragraph. This is done simply with the following code:

```
<center><hr width=75% border=3 color=<?php echo $bordercolor ?>></center>
```

To embed a video, copy the embed code from YouTube to your clipboard. Type the following code (typically the video will be place at the end of your article - but type the code where ever you want to embed the video):

```
<br><center><!- - embed code goes here - -></center><br>
```

Remember, <br> creates a blank line. You may want to add an additional <br> either before, after or both to create a double line skip. View your page and see how it looks.

Putting the finishing touches on the left column article, I typically highlight all uses of the primary keyword throughout the article (not the headings) using the BOLD tag. Simply locate all instances of your primary keyword in the article and enclose the keyword between the opening and closing BOLD tags (...).

The next section of code opens up and defines the second column (<td>) of the page:

```
<td width="250" style="border-left: groove 5px <?php echo $bordercolor ?>" valign="top">
```

In our left column, the first element to appear is an image. One inserts an image and defines its size using the <img> tag:

```
<!-- Page 1 Image and Alternate Text -->

<center><img src="<?php echo $url ?>/images/<?php echo $page1image ?>" height="235"
width="225"></center>
<br>
```

Note that the image in the code is a PHP variable ($). In the template all of the image file names are inserted in the config.php file. Images are uploaded into the images FOLDER.

Underneath the image I have placed the Facebook "like" button. The code is as follows:

```
<center>
<div class="fb-like" data-href="<?php echo $url ?>" data-width="200"
data-layout="button_count" data-action="like" data-show-faces="false"
data-share="true"></div>
 <br>
```

Then I place a single line dividing line:

```
<center><hr width=75% border=3 color=<?php echo $bordercolor ?>></center>
<br>
```

Next, you can decide if you want to promote a Clickbank or Amazon or other affiliate product on your page. The product/service you promote should relate to the subject of your article. With Clickbank, you can code in an image of the product with your affiliate link underneath. You code in a link as follows:

```
<a href="<!- - Paste your affiliate link here - ->" target="_blank">Click Here</a>
```

The statement "target='_blank'" opens the link in a new tab so that the visitor does not totally leave your website.

If you want the image itself to also be a link, use the <a ...> tag to enclose the <img> tag as follows:

```
<a href="<!- - Your Affiliate Link - ->" target="_blank"><img src="images/...." height="..."
width="..."></a>
```

The code assumes that the image file has been uploaded into your images folder of your directory. You can specify the height and width of the image to your liking (in pixels). For example: height="100" width="85" . You do not use the pixel notation (px).

Amazon has a display widget and gives you code to embed. Just embed it between <center> tags:

```
<center><!- - The Amazon Product embed HTML code goes here - - ></center>
```

After the affiliate product, I place another dividing line:

```
<br>
<center><hr width=75% border=3 color=<?php echo $bordercolor ?>></center>
<br>
```

Last in the right column on the index ("Home") page of my information websites I try to put an RSS Feed. RSS means "Real Simple Syndication." An RSS feed can either be a news feed or an article feed. Typically, I use the ezinearticles.com article feed provided I can find a feed relative to the subject of my website.

Remember? A "good" website has content that is regularly updated and maintained. Well, in all likelihood you are not going to want to regularly re-write your articles (not after you put all of that work into them placing keywords and otherwise composing it). An RSS feed IS regularly updated as new news or articles become available. By placing a feed on your site, it helps to satisfy this requirement. The feed as it appears on your website is not static, it will appear with new news or articles on a regular basis.

The most search engine friendly way of placing an RSS feed on your website is using the PHP code, which I included in the template:

```php
<?php
    $rss = new DOMDocument();

    /* Replace and paste the URL to your RSS feed between the 'http://feeds...' in the $rss->
statement below */

    $rss->load('http://feeds.ezinearticles.com/category/Computers-and-Technology:Progra
mming.xml');



    $feed = array();
    foreach ($rss->getElementsByTagName('item') as $node) {
        $item = array (
            'title' => $node->getElementsByTagName('title')->item(0)->nodeValue,
            'desc' =>
$node->getElementsByTagName('description')->item(0)->nodeValue,
            'link' => $node->getElementsByTagName('link')->item(0)->nodeValue,
            'date' =>
$node->getElementsByTagName('pubDate')->item(0)->nodeValue,
            );
        array_push($feed, $item);
    }
    $limit = 5;
    for($x=0;$x<$limit;$x++) {
        $title = str_replace(' & ', ' &amp; ', $feed[$x]['title']);
        $link = $feed[$x]['link'];
        $description = $feed[$x]['desc'];
        $date = date('l F d, Y', strtotime($feed[$x]['date']));
        echo '<p><strong><a href="'.$link.'" title="'.$title.'"
target="_blank">'.$title.'</a></strong><br />';
        echo '<small><em>Posted on '.$date.'</em></small>';
        echo '<p>'.$description.'</p>';
    }
?>
```

The problem with the PHP code is that it may not always work. Sometimes, ezinearticles blocks the IP of a web hosting service's server for what it feels are security reasons and the DOM - $rss->load code that is required fails. The solution to this is to use an RSS widget from an outside source. I have located a free RSS feed widget site, the link to which can be found connected to a pink button link toward the bottom on the right hand side of the "Getting Started" page of the CCC online course.

To display an RSS feed, what you need is the XML URL. To obtain the XML URL of an ezine articles article feed for your niche, go to the ezine articles RSS feed listing (the link to which is on the right hand side of the "Getting Started" page of the CCC online course). Locate the article niche you want, click on it, then click "XML".

The XML of the feed will open in a new tab. All you need is the URL as it appears in your browser's address bar. Copy it to your clipboard.

I place either the widget or the PHP code for my RSS feeds between a little header and HTML code as follows:

```
<center><b>'Of Interest' Articles:</b><br><br><small><small>

<!- - insert the embed code for the widget or code the PHP RSS read code here - - >

</small></small></center>
```

That completes my index page, so the next code simply entails closing out the right column </td> and closing out the structural table for the page:

```
</td>
</tr>
</table>
</center>
```

~

REMEMBER TO "SAVE" YOUR WORK WHEN YOU ARE FINISHED AND ALSO INTERMITTENTLY WHILE YOU ARE WORKING "JUST IN CASE" SOMETHING SHOULD HAPPEN EITHER WITH YOUR INTERNET OR THE HOSTING COMPANY WEBSITE.

~ *Intermission* ~

We have come to an intermission in the lecture series.

During this time, you should be able to insert your content on pages 2 and 3 of your website (your supporting articles). The only difference between the index page and pages 2 and 3 is that on pages 2 and 3 you will not have your star rating, the Facebook "like" button code or an RSS feed. You can promote different affiliate products if you want to. Remember your "includes":

```php
<?php
include "top.php";
?>



<?php
include "bottom.php";
?>
```

...and to BOLD your primary keywords throughout your articles.

When you are finished with pages 2 and 3, you should go to the Custom Code Cash online course and catch up, if you have not gone through the online course already. Read through the "Getting Started" page and the "Course Home" page. On the "Course Home" page, you should have read through the "Preliminaries."

After the CCC online course "catch-up," you should be able to complete your config.php file variables: your site colors, the titles for your navigation buttons, and inputting your image filenames. Images you select should be uploaded into your images FOLDER. Remember, filenames are case sensitive and the images should be typed in with the inclusion of the file extention (.png, .jpg, .gif etc.).

At this point, you can also return to the top.php file and type in a brief description of your website and type in ALL of your keywords, comma separated, in the META tags.

Lecture 14 - Background

You "style" your website's background in the style.php file. There are 3 variations to "background" that you can choose from:

1) Solid Color Background;
2) Repeating Image Background, with out without a Solid Color behind the image;
3) Single Image Background that spans the background/window.

In the template is the following style coding for the HTML document "body":

```
body {

 background: url() no-repeat center center fixed;
          -webkit-background-size: cover;
          -moz-background-size: cover;
          -o-background-size: cover;
          background-size: cover;
          background-size: 100% 100%;
          background: <?php echo $backgroundcolor ?>;
color: black;

}
```

It is not exactly correct and you should modify the code if you opt for options 2 or 3 as your background.

The simple code for a solid color background is:

```
body {

background: <?php echo $backgroundcolor ?>;
color: black;

}
```

The statement "color: black" is not the background, it is the color of the text as it will appear on the pages.

Option 2 is a repeating image background, with or without a solid color behind the image (in case you are using a vector graphic). The body style would appear as follows:

```
body {

background: <?php echo $backgroundcolor ?> url(images/{the filename of your background image});
background-size: 300px 300px;
color: black

}
```

You can modify the image size to your suiting. Just change the "300px 300px" to whatever "px" you want.

For option 3, a single image background that spans the entire background/window, the code is as follows:

```
body {

background: url(images/{the filename of your background}) no-repeat center center fixed;
        -webkit-background-size: cover;
        -moz-background-size: cover;
        -o-background-size: cover;
        background-size: cover;
        background-size: 100% 100%;
color: black;

}
```

Decide on the background you want and modify the body style code in the style.php file as necessary. The default for the template is a solid color background.

Lecture 15 - about.php File

A "good" website has both AUTHORITY and PURPOSE. These are the declarations that are made on the "About" page.

YOU are the author and authority, but you must indicate what makes you such. Perhaps you have a degree in the subject or perhaps you are just a subject enthusiast. Either way, SOMETHING has to be stated to show others that you have some AUTHORITY to be writing on the topic at hand.

Your website must also have a PURPOSE other than selling affiliate products. The purpose could be to present a hypothesis or to inform visitors of an alternative approach to take on a subject...or simply to bring to light things that may not be common knowledge. Think of it that the visitor has a purpose for visiting the site - to gain some insight or information - state how you are satisfying the visitor's desire for that insight or information.

Like the other pages, I set the about page also as a 2 column page. The entire code for the page (as it appears in the template) is as follows:

(about.php) _____

```php
<?php
include "top.php";
?>
<br>
<center><table width="900"><tr>

<td width="650">
<div style="margin-left: 15px;margin-right: 15px">

<!-- 'About' Article -->


<center><h1>About</h1></center>
```

```
<p>{Your Name} is a {site subject enthusiast/degree/authority} and the creator of
this website.  The
purpose of this website is {briefly describe the website purpose/benefit to
visitor}.</p>



<br>
</div>
</td>

<td width="250" style="border-left: groove 5px <?php echo $bordercolor ?>"
valign="top">

<!-- 'About' Image and Alternative Text -->

<center><img src="<?php echo $url ?>/images/<?php echo $aboutimage ?>"
alt="Patti Markow" height="235" width="225"></center>
<br>
</td>
</tr>
</table>
</center>
<?php
include "bottom.php";
?>
```

You can keep your "About" article as simple as indicated in the template code or
you can expatiate further. The image I typically use on my "About" page is an
image of myself. For the alternate image text, of course you would put YOUR
name in place of my name.

Lecture 16 - contact.php File

Since you are not asking for money from your visitor or selling a product as an e-commerce vendor, your "contact" information need only be as plain and simple as an email address. If you WERE asking for money, you should also include a physical address and, perhaps, a phone number as part of your contact information.

A word on the email address:

You basically would not want to use your personal email address as the contact. You could end up getting a lot of crank and spam emails. Personally, I don't like to be so public with my personal email address.

What I typically do is open a new Google gmail account for EACH ONE of my websites (this comes in handy later, as well). I put the new gmail email address as my contact email address and have the mail from that account FORWARDED to my personal email address. This way, I do not receive the spam that may go to that account and I usually only receive what are, more or less, the important or significant emails.

As with the other pages, the contact page is also a 2 column page. With the template, I included a default image - which you can change by changing the file name for the contact page image in the config.php file.

The code looks like this:

(contact.php)
_____

```php
<?php
include "top.php";
?>
<br>
<center><table width="900"><tr>

<td width="650">
<div style="margin-left: 15px;margin-right: 15px">
```

```
<!-- Contact Information -->


<center><h1>Contact</h1></center>
<center>
<p>You can contact this site's owner anytime via email at:</p>
<br>
<h2 style="text-shadow: 1px 1px <?php echo $bordercolor
?>">your-email@gmail.com</h2>
</center>
<br>
<br>
</div>
</td>

<td width="250" style="border-left: groove 5px <?php echo $bordercolor ?>"
valign="top">

<!-- Contact Image and Alternative Text -->

<center><img src="<?php echo $url ?>/images/<?php echo $contactimage ?>"
alt="Contact" height="235" width="225"></center>
<br>
</td>
</tr>
</table>
</center>

<?php
include "bottom.php";
?>
```

If you read through the code it is basically straight forward. Feel free to modify the text if you want to.

Lecture 17 - Site Completion

You should be ready, at this point, to complete your first website. Your style.php and config.php files should be finished. Your top.php should be completed with regard to site description and keywords. Your content and images should be in place. You should have your affiliate products promoted in the right hand columns, if you decide to promote affiliate products. You should have your RSS feed in place, your colors set and your site pretty much finished.

For the steps to complete the website, I refer you once again to the Custom Code Cash online course - "Course Home" page - "Site Completion" section.

When you have executed those steps, we will put some finishing touches on our website.

Lecture 18 - Website Banner

What I like to do, even for my information/article websites, is create a 468x60 banner for the purpose of promotion - or just to have ready in the event I decide to promote.

Here is an example of a 468x60 banner for an information site:

I house the banner image on the bottom of my "About" page as many times the advertising website requires the banner image URL, which does not exist unless the banner is uploaded to the website file directory - and also for ease of copying the banner image URL.

It takes just a few minutes to create a banner, like the one above. I use the Banner Ad Creator for the background and placing the image on the banner (the link to this tool is found near the bottom of the pink link buttons on the "Getting Started" page of the CCC online course) and Lunapic (pink link button also on the "Getting Started" page of the online course) for adding the words. Lunapic has a larger selection of fonts and placement of the words and phrases is a lot simpler.

Note that I put the permanent URL on the banner. Including the website www address is not a REQUIREMENT but it is a good idea so that people viewing the banner can SEE as well as being linked to the web address when you promote.

To display your banner on your "About" page, code in the following after your "about" paragraph:

```
<br><br>
<center><img src="images/{ filename of your uploaded banner }" height="60"
width="468"></center>
<br><br>
```

There are two statistics that I like to track on my websites: Total Visits and Visitors Online. To track these stats for me, I use a free service called "Shiny Stat."

You can find the pink link button for Shiny Stat in the "Extras" section on the "Getting Started" page of the CCC online course.

The one thing I do not like about Shiny Stat is that you need to use a different email address and sign up for another account for EVERY website you want to place a Shiny Stat widget on. But hence, the other reason for creating a new gmail account for every one of the websites I create.

After you sign up for the account and are ready to get the embed code, select the second embed code option - the one for code WITHOUT javascript.

You place the code in the right column of your structural table, above the advertisements, in the bottom.php file.

```
<!-- Adsense 120 x 240 Ads -->

<td valign="top">
<br>
<!-- Begin ShinyStat Free code -->
<div align=center>
<a href="https://www.shinystat.com" target="_top">
<img src="https://noscript.shinystat.com/cgi-bin/shinystat.cgi?USER=jobcompensation"
alt="Blog counters" border="0" /></a>
</div>
<!-- End ShinyStat Free code -->

<br>
```

The <td> (column opener) for the second column is a little ways down in the code. It is after your website footer (the copyright table) and just above where you should place the code for your ad zones. You can spot it by the opening <td valign="top">.

Lecture 20 - Border Image

On my company website I added a finishing touch that you might want to do on your website, or perhaps a future website: I added a border image.

Adding a border image is simple code.

First, you have to find a border image. For this I refer you to Pixabay and in the search box type "picture borders". You will see border images like the one I chose:

"Save Picture As...", then upload it into the images folder of your website directory. Then open the top.php file. Locate your main site definition table. The code will look something like this:

```
<!-- Main Site Definition Table -->

<td>

<center><table width="900"><tr><td bgcolor=<?php echo $sitecolor ?>
style="border-radius: 50px">
        <div style="border: groove 35px <?php echo $bordercolor ?>;border-radius:
50px">
        <div style="border: groove 35px <?php echo $bordercolor ?>;border-image:
url(images/denizenborder.png) 30 stretch; border-width: 50px;border-radius: 50px;
        -webkit-border-image: url(images/denizenborder.png) 30 stretch;
   -o-border-image: url(images/denizenborder.png) 30 stretch;
   -moz-border-image: url(images/denizenborder.png) 30 stretch;
   ">
```

The <div...> definition that I added to make the border image is colored purple. You replace the "denizenborder.png" image filename with the filename of the border image you selected.

You also have to code the closing </div> in the bottom.php file:

```
<center><font id="fontz2" size=4 color=<?php echo $sitecolor ?>><b>Copyright <?php echo
date(Y)." " ?> - Denizen-House Enterprises - All Rights Reserved</b></font></center>
    </td></tr></table></center>
<br>
</div>
</div>




</td>
```

~ *Conclusion* ~

This concludes the first lecture series of Custom Code Cash. I hope you learned a lot and now feel comfortable working with a web host and website files and folders. It is really nothing to be afraid of. Most mistakes can be corrected or, at worse, you just end up having to re-code. That is why you should save your work not just when you are finished, but intermittently while you are working.

In conjunction with the Custom Code Cash online course you should now have at your disposal all of the information you need and links to resources so that you can continue with your experience at custom coding websites. Whether it be for just a hobby or you want to create an enterprise, that makes either passive income from affiliate sales and advertising by keeping your websites or creating websites specifically to sell, I hope you will discover as I did that it is enjoyable, challenging and work where you are constantly learning.

Don't forget to visit W3Schools (the link you will find on the "Getting Started" page of the online course). They are always updating as code changes or new versions of code come into existence. I refer to the website constantly, for a quick reminder or to learn something new.

And don't forget to write down all of your questions. If you still have questions that are unanswered by these lectures, send me an email. Later editions of this series will have a "Frequently Asked Questions" section not included here in this first edition. I am always available to help and will respond as soon as feasibly possible.

denizenhouse@gmail.com

My name is Patti Markow.

~ *Notes* ~

~ *Notes* ~

~ *Notes* ~

~ *Notes* ~

~ *Notes* ~

~ Notes ~

www.ingramcontent.com/pod-product-compliance
Lightning Source LLC
Chambersburg PA
CBHW050934060326
40690CB00039B/488